WHERE MYTH AND HISTORY MEE⊕

A Christian Response to Myth

Craig Payne

University Press of America,® Inc.
Lanham · New York · Oxford

Copyright © 2001 by
University Press of America,® Inc.
4720 Boston Way
Lanham, Maryland 20706
UPA Acquisitions Department (301) 459-3366

12 Hid's Copse Rd.
Cumnor Hill, Oxford OX2 9JJ

Library of Congress Cataloging-in-Publication Data

Payne, Craig.
Where myth and history meet : a Christian response
to myth / Craig Payne.
p.   cm
Includes bibliographical references and index.
1. Myth. 2. History—Religious aspects—Christianity.
3. Truth—Religious aspects—Christianity. I. Title.

BR135 .P35 2001   230—dc21   2001053076 CIP

ISBN 0-7618-2148-1 (pbk. : alk. paper)

⊖™ The paper used in this publication meets the minimum
requirements of American National Standard for Information
Sciences—Permanence of Paper for Printed Library Materials,
ANSI Z39.48—1984

For Nathan Thomas Payne
and
Erin Elizabeth Payne

Contents

Preface

In this book, I argue for a certain view of the relationship between mythic stories and religious stories. More particularly, I argue for this view as it applies to the relationship between myth and Christianity, especially as we examine the central stories of Christianity, the stories regarding Christ as found in the Gospels. This view is one I share, to one degree or another, with two other writers whose work has been helpful to me, Mircea Eliade and C.S. Lewis. At first glance, these two might seem to have little in common; however, Eliade's researches into the sociology of religion and Lewis's literary and social criticism, as well as his religious apologetics, do often overlap in their discussions of myth. I would like to freely acknowledge my profound indebtedness to them at the beginning. Without their work, this book would not exist, at least not in its present form. They, "being dead, yet liveth."

As I present my central argument, I also briefly argue against two other views of the relationship between myth and religion, or myth and Christianity: (1) the view that biblical writings are to be accepted in their entirety as straightforward history, with no regard to their mythic content or parallels; and (2) the view that biblical writings (especially the Gospels) are simply another form of myth, with no regard to their presentation as factual history. Opposed to these views, I argue that Christianity itself is a *sui generis* phenomenon: the union of mythic saga with historical narrative, the eternal Word which became flesh.

Even in the making of a book as short as this one, the aid of many people is invaluable and should be mentioned. I would like to thank the following: Diana Lavery of the University Press of America, for her assistance; Dr. Jim Barnes of Truman State University, for the introduction to myth studies; Dr. Richard Fumerton of the University of Iowa, for the discussions on epistemology; the staff and fellow faculty members of Indian Hills Community College, for the congenial and stimulating atmosphere in which to work; department head Rhonda Eakins, for her interest, support, and thought-provoking conversations; pastors Larry and Nancy Ulrich, for their wise guidance; and finally, my wife, Desirae, and children, Nathan and Erin, for their unfailing love and patience.

August 2001

Introduction

Pictures in the Clouds

At the conclusion of Wallace Stevens's wonderful little poem, "The Snow Man," these lines occur:
> . . . For the listener, who listens in the snow,
> And, nothing himself, beholds
> Nothing that is not there and the nothing that is. (1:10)

This book will primarily be concerned with examining this paradox, that of the "nothing that is not there" and the "nothing that is," in the light of religious faith.

Let me illustrate this: When we lie on our backs in a soft spring meadow and gaze at the bulging clouds overhead, we literally see "nothing that is not there." All we see, in other words, are certain cloud formations, formations caused by atmospheric conditions which doubtless could be explained readily enough by a meteorologist. This meteorologist could explain to us how clouds are formed by water or ice particles, how they can be categorized into four families and approximately ten types, and so on. These particle formations are what we see with our physical eyes as we look at clouds, and we see nothing else; we see "nothing that is not there."

But, in our experience, is that really all we see in the clouds? Do we not usually see much more? Do we not see castles in the air, great horses and fantastic beasts, cavalry charges and clashes between titanic armies? Do we not see gigantic faces, forms, gods and demons in the upper atmosphere? Have not all of us had these or similar experiences when gazing at the clouds? And are these visions "nothing"?

Yes, they are literally "nothing"; however, they are the "nothing that is." In other words, they are the *artistic illusions* that are nonetheless *real to us as we see and accept them.*

The Nothing that Is

In Wallace Stevens's poem, this artistic illusion, the "nothing that is," seems to give meaning and purpose to the one who accepts the illusion (the "listener"). In fact, Stevens seems to suggest further that all meaning, purpose, or understanding in "reality" (the "nothing that is not there") arises by means of this artistry, this illusion, this "nothing that is." This artistic illusion, then, might be described as a *myth*—that is, an artistic story purporting to explain the fundamentals of human existence: the mysteries of our origin, our purpose, our "meaning" in life, and so on.

To Stevens, then, it appears that the "nothing that is" is real, is actually something—but perhaps real only to the one seeing it. The "vision" is real, but also subjective. And this is where orthodox Christianity begins to question the image of the "nothing that is." For if this image were true, would not Christianity, or indeed all religious faith, itself be only a form of the "nothing that is"? Would it not be merely an artistic illusion, an illusion that is nonetheless real to the one accepting it in active, imaginative faith? Would the words "Jesus is Lord" or "Christ is risen" have any real, objective meaning outside of the "myth" or fundamental story which is accepted by Christians to explain the universe and their places in it?

The response of orthodox Christianity has been to stress the objective nature of the Christian story. (Contrary religious views of myth, such as that held by Rudolf Bultmann and his followers, will be discussed briefly in a later chapter.) Christianity holds that Christian faith lies in objective, historical certainties, and not merely in subjective belief; Christianity's connection "with a historical event and Person," as theologian Emil Brunner writes, is "indispensable" (2:14). Often the Christian accepts the stories of the divinity of Christ, His redemptive work, and His resurrection and ascension first and foremost as *facts*, to be accepted in the same spirit as the statement, "Lincoln was assassinated in Ford's Theater" or "Wallace Stevens was an American poet."

On the other hand, Christianity today, because of this stance, has been accused by many of degenerating into a bloodless, over-intellectualized rationalism, a dry, dusty, historical artifact which perhaps appeals to certain intellects but has nothing for the living spiritual needs of the day. "It's all well and good to deny the validity of the subjective vision," the critic might say, "but what does Christianity offer in its place? A set of historical statements to memorize? A catechism? Statements which you either accept as 'factual' or else be damned?" A "do-it-yourself" spirit—make up your own religion as you go along—has consequently infiltrated the religious atmosphere, along with a sort of practical atheism which does not so much repudiate Christianity as ignore its claims. Many question: Where is the living spirit behind the letter of religious doctrine?

The Shaping Function of Art

To many serious artists, such as Stevens, the answer lies in the creative power of redemptive myth-making. The real conflict of life is a conflict of visions; it is the vision of mythic order against the vision of life's meaninglessness. In this artistic view, there is no *real* order to life to be found in nature; there is, after all, "nothing that is not there." However, the artist *imposes* order upon chaos and actually creates purpose for the spiritual life by the act of imagination, the act of imposing pattern upon life's monstrous and apparent irrationality. The artist, in the words of the late novelist John Gardner, creates a "rationale" for "heroism" and "the feeling of tribal unity. . . . And sure, it's a lie, but it's also a vision" (3:179). Art takes the place of religion, or rather transmutes itself into religion, since both are inherently visionary and revelatory. In this heavily romanticized view of art, the artist is supremely influential and so carries a heavy moral responsibility to be "true" to himself and his art; he is the true legislator of humanity, as Shelley believed.

Literary critic Helen Vendler, in the videotape series *Voices and Visions*, speaks of this imposition of pattern and order in her comments on Wallace Stevens's poem "The Idea of Order at Key West," in particular these lines:

She was the single artificer of the world
In which she sang. And when she sang, the sea,
Whatever self it had, became the self
That was her song, for she was the maker . . .
. . . .

. . . there never was a world for her
Except the one she sang and, singing, made.
. . . .
Oh! Blessed rage for order . . .
The maker's rage to order words . . . (1:129-30)

In commenting on "The Idea of Order," Vendler points out "the way
the poet *charts* the world for us, just the way geographers chart the
world by making up those imaginary lines like the equator and
longitude and latitude lines," and goes on to say,

None of those are real; you can't see those lines . . . but nonetheless
it's by longitude and latitude lines that we give our position in
relation to the world. And it's that that the poet does, too. . . . After
we listen to the artist, suddenly the world appears charted as if by
new lines of latitude and longitude . . ., the world becomes
intelligible, rather than the random mass of sensation our senses
receive. . . . All organization of nature into culture does this. (4:)

The shaping artist, in this view, affirms order, the order to which we all
intuitively respond. The artist's central problem then is not the truth of
doctrinal statements, but rather involves the definition and description
of this order in aesthetically "true" forms, forms which often defy
systematic articulation, though they are encountered in the forms of
everyday reality—and so it is to the imposed order of art, the "imitation
of reality," that we turn for the parameters and standards of organized
culture.

Order: Imposed or Reflected?

This artistic vision of the world of order seems to repudiate the
opposing vision of a world of chaos. However, it is important to
remember that the artist's order-giving symbols are not recognized by
anything in nature except humanity, but are put forward by the artist,
the Order-Giver who is imposing pattern on the seeming chaos of life.

For example, whatever else one might think about the validity or
lack thereof of the zodiacal symbols, the fact remains that many
throughout history have found order and meaning in the patterns
brought out by whatever artist first looked at the scattered stars and saw
pictures. If comfort and purpose have been found by many in tales of
the remote stars, how much more so in the stories of a kind, all-
knowing, all-powerful Creator, stories which reflect the natural
symbols of Father, Leader, spiritual Family, and so on?

So the ambiguity of the artist's vision is also the ambiguity of the
religious vision. We must first of all ask ourselves, Do we believe in

the meaninglessness of existence or in the meaning imposed by mythic patterning, by artistic illusion? What does it mean to "believe" in an illusion, in the "nothing that is"? And, more importantly for our purposes: Is this what we mean when we talk of religious belief?

For this line of thinking leads directly to a second question for the religious believer: *What is the nature of what we believe?* Do we believe in what well-known apologist C.S. Lewis calls "the True Myth," in the idea that "the pattern is there in Nature because it was first there in God" (5:116)? Does meaningful pattern in nature even exist, or does the mythic artist construct and impose meaning rather than reflect the meaningful pattern already present? And does this distinction ultimately matter? In other words, does the reality behind the patterning transcend the myths devised by the patterners?

Another way of asking the same question is this: Is the religious vision grounded in a reality beyond our artistic imaginations? Or is it merely a more fundamental and aesthetically powerful "illusion," as Freud calls religion—a sort of glorified "picture in the clouds"?

In this book, I would like to explore these questions regarding the relationship of myth and Christianity, first by introducing and examining several contrasting views of this relationship, and then by presenting what I regard as the most satisfactory Christian view of these problems—the view in which myth and history meet and merge.

Chapter 1

Myth and the Central Questions

Myth studies seem to be everywhere nowadays. The two-year college at which I teach offers in its curriculum "Myth and Literature" in addition to the more typical World Lit. and American Lit. courses; a school in a neighboring town not only offers a similar course, but also a basic course in mythology for undergraduates and a course, "Studies in Myth," for the more advanced student. In higher education itself, Northrop Frye's theories of literary analysis by way of myth permeate the intellectual atmosphere, or at least the somewhat rarefied atmosphere with which I am most familiar, that of the English department. On television, we see George Lucas of *Star Wars* fame discussing the influence of myth on his films. Even in the mail this week, all of the book club catalogs I received include sections on myth, usually incorporated with the religion / philosophy / spirituality sections; in fact, these sections are so well established by now that they are sub-specialized into feminist myth studies, Native American myth studies, comparative myth studies, myth theory, and so on.

This recent surge of popularity of myth studies may be attributed to the fact that ours is a relentlessly questioning age, and myth studies purport to examine the central questions of life itself: Why are matters one way, and not another? What is the ground of our being, the ground of the universe we uneasily inhabit? What is the ground or rationale for the possibility of change within this being, within this universe? Does the possibility even exist? And if so, is this possibility of ultimate benefit, or is it just another random dance of atoms in the universal pageant? Why should the attempt at change even be made? The modern philosopher Eric Voegelin posits these questions as the two principal questions of life, the questions of "existence" and "essence":

> The quest for the ground . . . is a constant in all civilizations. . . . The quest for the ground has been formulated in two principal questions of metaphysics. The first question is, "Why is there something; why not nothing?" and the second is, "Why is that something as it is, and not different?" (1:2)

Because of his human ancestry, because of his part in the world-*Logos* or ordering principle which makes the chaotic universe into a cosmological vision, the generic human "does not live in order to live, he wants to know why and for what he lives," according to theologian Emil Brunner (2:54). Before the possibility of self-sacrifice in seeking the true, the good, and the beautiful for its own sake and not for its potential usefulness is chosen, this human cannot help looking for the meaning, even eternal meaning, and ground behind existence: "He recognizes not only that there is something, but that something ought to be. He not only sees a reality but tries to see a meaning for what is real" (2:55).

In other words, humans eternally ask the question: What is life's purpose? The recent emphasis on myth studies seems to be another manifestation of that persistent query. Myth *does* appear to organize existence into purposeful categories; however, if life truly *has* no purpose (meaning an objective purpose outside of the mere facticity of "what occurs"), then is not all of the orchestration and organization of meaningful pattern done by the myth-maker also purposeless, no matter how skillfully wrought or how many "believe in" the artistic contrivance? Is any sort of imposition of meaning a construction of whole cloth rather than a reflection of reality—or, more bluntly, is it a cold-blooded lie? Is myth purely social in function and origin, the "useful lies" of the clerics and artists merely a form of social cement to bind the masses into the coherent enterprise of society?

And so, even at the very beginning of our look at modern myth studies, we come inescapably to the question of religious truth.

The Inescapable Issue

"To my way of thinking," writes David Bidney, "the central and inescapable issue is the relevance of the question of truth to mythic belief." Bidney goes on to say:

If myth be conceived as an intrinsically subjective mode of experience, then it may be said to have a purely psychological and ethnological value as a record and expression of uncritical, "physiognomic" emotional experience. The "truth" of myth would then lie in its factual and historical subjectivity. But if the mythic and religious intuition of the solidarity and continuity of cosmic life be accepted as true in the sense of *being in accord with a non-mythic reality*, then myth may be interpreted allegorically. . . . The truth of myth is then a function of the interpretation of myth. If one accepts the truth of the original intuition of the solidarity of life and the dramatic character of its underlying forces, then myth symbolizes allegorically a fundamental metaphysical and religious truth. For the sociological approach, however, the truth of myth consists in its symbolic expression of ritual and has no cosmic reference. (3:15-16, emphasis added)

Probably chief today among these "symbolists" Bidney describes who hold that myth has no actual "cosmic reference" is the prolific writer and scholar Joseph Campbell, whose influence seems to have expanded since his death in 1987. Campbell's books, in particular *The Power of Myth*, a compilation of interviews conducted by Bill Moyers, are best-sellers today, especially on college campuses; the video interviews with Moyers have been repeatedly broadcast on public television and, along with another series of videotaped lectures of Campbell (*The World of Joseph Campbell*), are often presented in classes on psychology, history, sociology, anthropology, myth studies, religion, world literature, and so on. Therefore, perhaps a closer examination of some of Campbell's views would help us, chiefly by way of contrast, to set out a distinct alternative to the purely "symbolic" view of myth.

Most students or others reading his books or viewing the videotapes will doubtless think of Campbell as a path-breaking pioneer shedding the old, worn-out straitjacket of religious dogma and finding the mystical truth at the heart of reality. On the other hand, others see in Campbell yet another manifestation of an ancient, discredited (but persistent) Gnostic intellectual system which specifically *denies* reality as it is given us to know it. One might even be so bold as to say that

Campbell is just another New Age-ish fad. But, as Owen Jones points out in a recent article on Campbell, "Many Americans, even devout Jews and Christians who ought to know better, often lack even the most basic spiritual and theological understanding that would help them handle the mysterious problems of pain, evil, suffering, and death. This spiritual illiteracy is the context in which the burgeoning interest in mythology and other forms of esoteric spirituality have begun to take on the form of a social movement complete with an intellectual system" (4:14).

Campbell's views of myth are considered "romantic" and not "sociological" by some critics (5:); however, I consider Campbell to fall squarely within the ranks of Bidney's "sociological" interpreters. In Campbell's own words, any search for "a meaning for life" is an illusion; rather, only "an experience of being alive" is of importance (6:5). Campbell rejects the ordering principle, the world-*Logos*, and so celebrates what Emil Brunner would label as *sub*-human, the human who lives merely "in order to live" (2:54). Therefore, though Campbell himself attacks those "literalists" who miss the "symbolic" truth of myth and are "going back to something that is vestigial" (6:12), he himself is the true "literalist" (the more exact philosophical label would be "materialist") in that, as Bidney rather neatly inverts it, he "does not acknowledge any reality other than symbolic reality" (3:15), symbolic reality being a function of the human mind.

Since the idea of a non-symbolic reality as a referent for myth is precluded, myth's function (no matter how often Campbell speaks of the "transcendental" or the "bliss" of mystical experience) becomes sociological and / or anthropological, i.e., "literal." Campbell's views therefore fit into a "sociological" view of myth, in which "not nature but society is the model for myth" (3:15).

The Authority of Myth

The question then confronting the student of myth is this: What is the source or authority or model of the social mythos? Or, to put the question another way, is the mythic vision of truth only valid insofar as it is socially useful, capable of creating cultural order and order-maintaining heroes? And if so, is this mythic vision of any real or ultimate value? What becomes of the Ultimate when its (or His) myths reflect only the human society which conceives it (or Him)?

To Campbell, of course, God Himself is the ultimate metaphor, as Campbell somewhat casually mentions from time to time in his teachings. "The reference of the metaphor in religious traditions is to something transcendent that is not literally any thing," he states in *The Power of Myth*:

> Every religion is true in one way or another. It is true when understood metaphorically. But when it gets stuck to its own metaphors, interpreting them as facts, then you are in trouble. (6:56)

By "literally" I take Campbell to mean "univocally" in the Thomist sense, i.e., language corresponding exactly or perfectly or in only one way to its object. By "thing" I assume is meant an object, or something material. If so, what Campbell presents is a platitude, but a platitude intended to have consequential effect; by saying the "transcendent" is "not literally any thing," Campbell actually intends to say, "The transcendent literally is not." As one writer has noted, Campbell has "an Emersonian gift for casting atheism in the language of faith" (7:50).

Nevertheless, admitting the analogical nature of religious language and denying its univocality (which admission and denial Aquinas made long ago) does not deny the *ens* or essential existence of the topics of language; admitting that language does not have a "literal" or even necessary relation to its object does not deny the "literalness" of the object itself. In more specific terms, admitting that our *predications* about concepts are essentially *analogical in nature* does not necessarily require us also to deny that the concepts themselves are essentially *unitary in meaning*.

(These questions of analogy, metaphor, and "literalness" really require a chapter in themselves. However, to insert this chapter would seem an interruption at this point. Therefore, for those interested, I offer the chapter "The Interaction of Experience and Language" as an appendix.)

Long before Campbell, G.K. Chesterton rather aptly described the Campbellian type of comparative mythologist: "They cannot believe that religion is really not a pattern but a picture. Still less can they believe that it is a picture of something that really exists outside our minds" (8:268).

Historical Revelation and the Christian Cult

For sociologically oriented myth theorists such as Campbell, the archetypal mythic pattern is a projection of human psychology, not a revelation of a non-symbolic reality. Therefore, in Campbell's view, Christians and Jews have for the most part missed the point, with their insistence on historical revelation; in particular, the notion of divine transcendence limiting itself in localized time and space is ridiculous, as, of course, Paul the apostle said it always would be (1 Cor. 1:23). In his best-known scholarly work, *The Hero with a Thousand Faces*, Campbell rejects "the concrete clutter of facts and events" (9:180) and asserts that "the knowledge of the transcendent principle" is "beyond the phenomenal realm of names and forms" (9:89); he believes that the notion of historical revelatory truth is the "blight" of the Bible and the "Christian cult" (9:249). Mythology, to Campbell as to Jung, is "psychology misread as biography" (9:256), and "the divine being" is "a revelation of the omnipotent Self, which dwells within us all"; we are called to "Know this and be God" (9:319).

It is important to recognize that to Campbell, and in the sociological approach in general, "the divine being" or "the transcendent" is merely this psychological principle; any evangelism to the contrary is "general propaganda," "superfluous," and "a menace" (9:390). This, of course, does not prevent his occasionally quoting from Jewish and Christian sources when they suit his purposes, since "truth" can break even out of "doctrine" at times. To Campbell, religious doctrine is concretized and therefore "ineffectual" myth (9:389); on the other hand, to the religious believer, the "doctrine" exists to balance truth with truth, the Campbellian grasp of "symbolic" truth with other truth more readily ignored, rejected, or misunderstood.

Others have also pointed out this misunderstanding and misrepresentation of Christian teaching, in even stronger terms than I am employing. For instance, educator and philosopher Mortimer Adler writes, "From what Campbell himself wrote on the subject, I can only conclude that his understanding of the Christian creed and its theology was puerile. In that field he was an ignoramus" (10:49). Elsewhere Adler summarizes Campbell's philosophical stance well:

> Professor Campbell was undoubtedly a very good social scientist in the field of cultural anthropology. But his competence in dealing with philosophical matters, especially in the field of philosophical theology, is highly questionable. His judgment in this area reflects the dogmatic materialism that is so prevalent in contemporary science, especially in the behavioral sciences. (11:60)

In his later years, Campbell, an ex-Catholic, himself admitted his actual relationship to the Christian faith: "Clearly Christianity is opposed fundamentally and intrinsically to everything that I am working and living for," he said, as quoted in a biography (12:414). Again, Chesterton is valuable here: "The worst judge of all is the man now most ready with his judgments: the ill-educated Christian turning gradually into the ill-tempered agnostic" (8:145).

So how does one rejecting the dogmatic materialism of the sociological approach to myth and open to the idea of religious truth approach the topic of myth?   Is the only Christian response to reject myth in its entirety?   Or is there a better, more meaningful response at hand?

Chapter 2

Should We Reject Myth Entirely?

The question stands before us: How does one rejecting the dogmatic materialism of the sociological approach to myth and open to the idea of religious truth approach the topic of myth? Before proceeding further, we should examine an alternative which bypasses any such approach whatsoever, the alternative, that is, of abandoning myth altogether as non-Christian and therefore irrelevant to the Christian faith and its teachings.

Such an alternative is usually based on passages from the Christian Testament such as 1 Timothy 1:4, in which the Greek word *mythos* is translated (in the King James Version) as "fables"; in fact, the KJV translates *mythos* as "fables" in all five places the word occurs in the Greek New Testament. In 2 Peter 1:16, *mythos* is specifically contrasted to the truth to be found in historical facts and dismissed summarily (1:381).

The article on *mythos* in Kittel and Friedrich's *Theological Dictionary of the New Testament* is equally dismissive. "Myth as such has no place on biblical soil," it states; ". . . . there is within it an inherent antithesis to truth and reality which is quite intolerable" (qtd. in 1:382). The author's conclusion is succinct: "The Christian Church, insofar as it is true to itself, accepts . . . that myth is untrue and consequently of no religious value" (qtd. in 1:381).

A first reaction to this might be to reconsider the tests of truth. Jesus said, for example, "I am the Door"; is this to be considered a lie? Before the quick response is made, "No, this is merely a metaphor, commonly used in teaching," it might be wise to consider the nature of metaphor. Or, to take a more extended example, Jesus told a story in which a sower sowed several types of ground with seed; the various plantings then met with highly specific fates. Is this a lie? Again, the response might be quick: "No, it is a parable, and was accepted as such by his hearers." But what are metaphors and parables if not non-factual, non-historical descriptions and stories? (Perhaps a better way of stating this would be to say that metaphors and parables do not *concern* themselves with fact or history as such.)

In fact, in his commentary on Genesis 1-11, Alan Richardson labels as "parables" the biblical stories of Creation, Cain and Abel, Noah's Flood, and so on. He argues, "Sometimes these stories are called 'myths,' but this word is open to serious misunderstanding" (2:27). Even in the scholarly usage of "myth" as "a story which is not literally true but which nevertheless contains a deep philosophical meaning" (2:27), we encounter problems. For example, to call the story of creation a "myth" should not be construed (as it doubtless would be by some) as saying that creation by God did not actually occur. As Richardson writes:

> The most that we can with propriety say is that the accounts of the Creation and Fall in Genesis are *mythical in form*; but since there is the ever-present danger that we shall be understood to mean that the Creation and Fall are "only myths," it is perhaps better to avoid the word altogether. We have adopted instead the word "parable." [In the present work, I shall continue to use the word "myth," while conceding Richardson's well-taken point—C.P.] .... A parable is a story which may or may not be literally true (no one asks whether the Good Samaritan ever literally "happened"); it conveys a meaning beyond itself. (2:28, emphasis in original)

So the test of "literalness" is not the only test of truth. If everything non-factual or non-historical is considered "untrue," antithetical to "truth and reality," or even "of no religious value," what are we to do with the parabolic and metaphoric teachings of Christ? Is there perhaps a further test of truth which these teaching methods would satisfy?

A Preparation for the Reality

A first reaction to myth, as we have seen, might be a reconsideration of the tests of truth. Secondly, we, along with many of the early Christian fathers, could consider universal archetypal patterns as the *praeparatio evangelica*, a preparation for the reality of the gospel to come—a preparation which loses none of its mythic radiance as it finds itself in historical manifestation. As Ernest F. Scott writes:

> In a larger sense the New Testament is to be considered historically. The church has always taken its stand on the great principle that the Word was made flesh, the Divine Life identified with humanity. But the implications of this truth used never to be fully grasped. It was assumed that the revelation broke in suddenly, and had nothing in common with anything that had gone before. We now recognize that although it was new it wove itself naturally into the existing life of the world. The forms in which it found expression had been prepared for it by an age-long process of development. Criticism . . . now takes full account of this historical preparation. . . . For centuries before Christ men had been "feeling after God if haply they might find him," and the new revelation attached itself to what was noblest and best in the world's earlier thought. (3:886-87)

By way of analogy, we might think of universal archetypes and mythic patterns as a sort of *glove*. A glove—no matter how closely it resembles a real hand—is not the hand itself. However, if not for that close resemblance to the hand, the glove would lose its point, its meaning. Similarly, myth (in a Christian view) must bear a close resemblance to the Christian reality. As the living reality of the hand fills (and fulfills the teleology of) the glove with its embodiment of the glove's pattern, so Christ fills and fulfills the mythic pattern. As C.S. Lewis puts it, "The old myth of the Dying God, *without ceasing to be myth*, comes down from the heavens of legend and imagination to the earth of history" (4:66, emphasis in original). If we may consider universal myth as part of the *praeparatio evangelica*, then we must also consider it part of God's evangel, the declaration of good tidings, before we consider that which makes the declaration itself particular and unique. The imaginative embrace must first be granted to the "forms" in which the Gospels "found expression," just as we grant it to any other literary artifact, before we see the distinctiveness which sets the Gospels apart, that which transcends the merely mythic.

To see this distinctiveness more clearly, let us first consider the differences between "traditional" and "abstract" art or literature. Traditional art is representational art. We might say, for instance, "This is a painting of a New York landscape" or, "This is the story of a one-legged sailor pursuing a white whale," and be reasonably sure of the artist's represented intent. But in the very act of representation, the artist has taken the first step, as Plato notes, away from the reality itself.

The representation is merely words on paper or streaks of paint on canvas, even though it may point toward a reality external to the artwork itself.

So what occurs when the streaks of paint represent nothing else, e.g., in abstract art, in which the art represents nothing external to itself? The romanticized view might say that this is the purest art, "art for art's sake." The traditional view might rather say that it is *design*, not art at all, merely an arrangement of line and color. However, if even traditional art is a step away from the reality itself, what else is it but also an arrangement of line and color? How can it be said to be different from abstract art?

The real difference seems to be one of *intent*, and therefore lifts traditional art into a different sphere than that which abstract art inhabits, a metaphysical sphere in which *final ends* are also considered (as the glove carries meaning because of its final end, the hand). Abstract art is mechanistic. Representing nothing external to itself, it also points to nothing but itself and signifies nothing but itself. This is why "art for art's sake" is ultimately lifeless and sterile, just as "sex for the sake of sex" is ultimately lifeless and sterile; both, if carried to their logical conclusions, end in solitary circularity. Anything considered only for itself becomes meaningless, except for that which is considered the ultimate good in itself, which in religious belief is God.

Traditional art, on the other hand, exists in at least two dimensions. It exists in the artistic realm and can be judged by the same standards of artistic merit as "art for art's sake." (In fact, it should be judged by these standards.) But it also exists as a pointer toward external reality, accepting reality as the *independent* character of that which is knowable, independent of the artwork itself. "A literary work belongs to God's created world," as Gallagher and Lundin state; "it is not an independent cosmos created only for pleasure. As part of God's world, works of literature are not mere language games but products of human beings who are deeply enmeshed in specific historical situations" (5:59).

The greatest art satisfies both of these standards, grounding itself both in the timeless artistic realm and in history; lesser art tends either toward the abstract (on the one hand) or the didactic (on the other). The same is true of literary art. Lesser literature tends toward the abstract (losing characters, plot, setting, etc., along the way, in the effort to "purify" the literary artifact) or toward the didactic and moralizing (which is likewise untrue to the paradoxical nature of human experience).

One interesting point about the mechanistic and materialistic world of "art for art's sake" is that it originally arose as a Romantic reaction against the very view of the world as a mechanism! However, in their deification of the human imagination, the Romantics effectively shut the door on anything *transcending* the merely human. We find art slowly becoming nothing more than the display of the products of one peculiar arrangement of mechanistic brain cells after another. And here is where our discussion makes its way back to myth; for we may say that, as the truest art transcends the merely artistic (without abandoning the artistic) when it points to a reality external to itself, so also a universal myth, such as the Dying God motif mentioned earlier, transcends the merely mythic (without abandoning the mythic) when it points to historical reality external to itself. As Scott says, the forms in which our Redemption found expression "had been prepared for it by an age-long process of development" (3:886). Like a hand slipping into a carefully prepared glove, the historical reality of Christ perfectly fulfills the mythic structures pointing toward Him.

(This is not to fall into Euhemerism, the view that mythic tales originate in some sort of historical incidents in the far-distant past. In fact, this view is the opposite of Euhemerism. Mythic patterns do not arise *out of* historical incidents; rather, they point *forward* to and find their fulfillment in historical reality.)

As we consider this point, we may perhaps take a further step. Should not we reconsider the literary *methods* of the Scriptures, and not merely their content?

Let us take the Book of Job as an example. Is it possible that this book, without compromise of faith, could be taken as an inspired story rather than as a history? If this idea cannot even be considered without jeopardizing the "truth" of the book, or even of the entire Bible, then I would ask once again, What were the metaphorical and parabolic teachings of Christ? Non-truth? Perhaps we must face a few more questions not typically found in explications of the Scriptures as a whole, e.g.: What constitutes "history"? And, once "history" is defined and the criteria for historical documents advanced (such as contemporaneity, first-hand testimony, primary sources, etc.), can we say that all of Scripture is strictly "history"? For instance, is there a difference *in kind* between Genesis 1-3 and the eyewitness, contemporarily written accounts to be found in the Gospels, wherein the Word becomes "flesh" and therefore bound within linear history? Does anything really happen to our doctrine of Scripture if we consider portions of that scripture as "inspired story" rather than as "inspired history"? If so, exactly what happens?

These questions, of course, are neither systematic nor exhaustive. But they are samples of the type of questions we must face as we consider the relationship of Christianity to myth (some of which will be taken up more fully in the next chapter). And please do not misunderstand me: I fully recognize that the Christ of the Gospels is not a philosopher. Neither is Moses; neither is Paul; neither are any of the prophets. Neither is Christianity to be considered a philosophical system. Neither do I advocate a philosophical or literary or aesthetic approach as a primary approach to the Bible. The Bible does not present itself as a book of philosophy, nor as literature; it presents itself unqualifiedly as the Word of God. But in so doing, it also inescapably raises questions which *are* both philosophical and literary in nature, and which require the tools of philosophy and literary analysis to probe.

The Abandoning of Universal Myth

A third reaction to the wholesale abandoning of myth lies in considering the scriptures upon which such an abandoning is based. For instance, referring to the word *mythos* in 1 Timothy 1:4, translated as "fables" in the King James Version, Greek scholar Marvin Vincent comments, "As to its reference here, it is impossible to speak with certainty [as to the type of myth indicated]" (qtd. in 6:27). He continues:

> Expositors are hopelessly disagreed, some referring it to Jewish, others to Gnostic fancies. It is explained as meaning traditional supplements to the law, allegorical interpretations, Jewish stories of miracles, Rabbinical fabrications, whether in history or doctrine, false doctrines generally, etc. (qtd. in 6:27)

The same authority also speaks of the connected word "genealogies" ("fables and endless genealogies") as possibly "the Gnostic *aeons* or series of emanations from the divine unity" or "genealogies as interpreted allegorically by Philo, and made the basis of a psychological system . . ." He also says the word "and" is explanatory: "The fables and genealogies form a single conception, the genealogies indicating in what the peculiarity of the fables consists" (qtd. in 6:27).

At any rate, the New Testament rejection of this form of *mythos* as unnecessary for salvation need not necessitate the wholesale abandoning of universal myth itself. The costs of this abandoning would seem to outweigh the benefits—even leaving aside the fact of myth's correspondence with the realities of our human experience, a correspondence to be explored in greater depth in the next chapter. The paradoxes of Christ already abound: the King who is also the Servant, the God who is also a man, the High Priest who is also the Sacrifice, the Great Shepherd who is also the Lamb, the Ancient of Days who is also the Child, the All-Powerful who is also the Suffering One. To this list we might add: the one found in Universal Myth who is also found in the localized history of a small piece of land in the Middle East—the Myth who is also fact.

Chapter 3

Myth and Religious Truth

The question we faced at the conclusion of Chapter 1 still stands before us, albeit in expanded form: How does one approach the topic of myth who (1) rejects the dogmatic materialism of the sociological approach to myth, (2) yet also rejects the wholesale abandoning of myth as "non-Christian," and (3) is open to the idea of religious truth?

We might begin by a proper understanding of certain key religious terms. To the religious person, the balance mentioned in Chapter 1, the balance of "symbolic" truth with "historic" truth to form "doctrine," can be and is occasionally expressed as a "complementarity," to use physicist Niels Bohr's term, or more frequently as "paradox." A paradox is something apparently absurd or incredible that may nonetheless be true; it is an attempt to hold simultaneously truthful propositions that appear on the surface to contradict each other. However, by "paradox" I do not mean logical contradictions such as (A & ~A), or, "It is the case that my name is Craig Payne and it is also not the case that my name is Craig Payne." What I *do* mean by "paradox" are propositions such as, "Whoever would save his life must lose it." This apparently absurd or contradictory statement could nonetheless be true, depending on what "saving" or "losing" one's life entails.

"Whether they are appraising the world or seeking to understand man's place in the cosmos," writes Reinhold Niebuhr, ". . . the wise men usually resolve the paradoxes of religion and arrive at a simpler and more consistent truth which has the misfortune of being untrue to the facts of human existence" (1:210-11). Niebuhr freely admits (quoting St. Paul), "We are deceivers, yet true, when we affirm that God became man to redeem the world from sin. The idea of eternity entering time is intellectually absurd" (1:13); yet he explains, "The Christian religion may be characterized as one which has transmuted primitive religious and artistic myths and symbols without fully rationalizing them" and goes on to say,

> Buddhism is much more rational than Christianity. In consequence Buddhism finds the finite and temporal world evil [as in the First Noble Truth—C.P.]. Spinozism is a more rational version of God and the world than the biblical account; but it finds the world unqualifiedly good and identical with God [as in Spinoza's famous *Deus sive natura*—C.P.]. (1:7)

If we may return for one moment to Joseph Campbell's theological thought, both of these rationalist themes (the unqualified evil of particularity / the unqualified goodness of universality) are apparent; he rejects the idea of finiteness and temporality inherent in Incarnation (the "concrete clutter of facts and events" [2:180]), yet accepts "the affirmation of all things": "Since in Hindu thinking everything in the universe is a manifestation of divinity itself, how should we say no to anything in the world?. . . . Who are we to judge? It seems to me that this is one of the great teachings, also, of Jesus" (3:67). Here Campbell misrepresents the Christian belief in the sacramental, incarnational universe. Christians do believe in the universe as a manifestation of the creative divine, but they also believe that humans can turn away from God's goodness and toward evil (evil being the lack or "privation" of goodness). Again, Campbell's materialist notions of "divinity" cause him to rationalize away the paradoxical point of Christian doctrine, that point which he then feels compelled to explain—to Christians.

"One of the most deplorable errors of symbolist theory," writes J.E. Cirlot in his invaluable *A Dictionary of Symbols*, ". . . lies in opposing the symbolical to the historical" (4:xiii). (We might recall Campbell's definition of religion as "psychology misread as biography" [2:256] for an example of this type of error.) Cirlot goes on:

> Arguing from the premise that there are symbols—and, indeed, there are many—which exist only within their own symbolic structure, the false conclusion is then drawn that all or almost all transcendental events which appear to be both historical and symbolic at once—in other words, to be significant once and for all time—may be seen

simply as symbolic matter transformed into legend and thence into history. (4:xiii)

"Both historical and symbolic at once"—"significant once and for all time"—such events, for the Christian, are to be found in the Gospels. Jesus Christ is the "bridge" between the two realities, to use Cirlot's word: "We can also see the ever-present possibility of a bridge linking both forms of reality in a cosmic synthesis" (4:xiv).

The Transcending of Myth

Of course, all Christians agree to a certain extent with Campbell's division between mythic or symbolic truth and the literal; as John Knox puts it in his book *Myth and Truth*, "the tests of truth are various" (5:18).   Knox argues through the idea of truth in "images" or metaphorical truth, but comes to a temporary halt: "The myth claims a kind of relation to objective, factual truth which other forms of allusive discourse do not claim" (5:23). After stumbling over Tillich's idea of "objective reference" and drawing from it the somewhat bland inference that "a myth is not an authentic myth if it is not believed" (5:27), Knox brings the point to a head: "How does one believe a myth?" (5:29).

In this, Knox follows Rudolf Bultmann, the primary Christian proponent of a "de-mythologized" Christianity; both believe that, as Bultmann writes, "myths give to the transcendent reality an immanent, this-worldly objectivity" (6:19), but depart from Christian orthodoxy in demanding that the myth of Christ be separate from the *kerygma* or announcement of this-worldly event.   Other Christians, as Knox concedes, insist to the contrary that "we cannot separate the proclamation that God acted in Christ from the story of what that action was" (5:47).

For example, C.S. Lewis maintains the union of myth and fact in Christ: "If ever a myth had become fact, had been incarnated, it would be just like this. . . . the myth must have become fact; the Word, flesh; God, man" (7:236). He explains himself more fully elsewhere:

As myth transcends thought, Incarnation transcends myth. The heart of Christianity is a myth which is also a fact. The old myth of the Dying God, *without ceasing to be myth*, comes down from the heavens of legend and imagination to the earth of history.   It *happens*—at a particular date, in a particular place, followed by definable historical consequences. . . . By becoming fact it does not cease to be myth; that is the miracle. . . . To be truly Christian we must both assent to the historical fact and also receive the myth (fact though it has become) with the same imaginative embrace which we accord to all myths. The one is hardly more necessary than the other. (8:66-67, emphasis in original)

Or, as Chesterton writes, "Unless these things are appreciated artistically they are not appreciated at all" (9:233).

It seems, then, that Lewis would not disagree with David Bidney, quoted in Chapter 1, but would perhaps rephrase Bidney's conception of a "non-mythic reality" into that of a mythic reality which also transcends the merely mythic or symbolic. In simpler terms, this would be a truly *transcendent* myth, or Myth, using "transcendent" in its classical and Christian sense and not in its sociological misuse as "immanent" or even "worldwide." As Cornelius Loew has noted, any religious "convictions," even in the very linguistic roots of the word, "point to someone or something . . . which is experienced as an exterior force by those who hold the conviction." This "experience from outside" is perceived as an "objective referent" to the one holding the convictions (10:3). Loew points out that the Hebrews and Greeks, in particular, maintained this conviction of transcendence or "apartness": "The life-orienting story that the Hebrews developed (sacred history) expressed the conviction that there is an ultimate other than man, society, or the cosmos" (10:5-6). Whether or not this "ultimate," this "objective referent," actually exists, it is important to note that in the dual tradition out of which Christianity grows the story or myth of divine action cannot be separated from the action itself. In other words, the mythic story is one with the historical account: "The Word became flesh, and dwelt among us" (John 1:14).

J.E. Cirlot is admirably direct on this matter: ". . . The symbolic in no way excludes the historical, since both forms may be seen . . . as functional aspects of a third: the metaphysical principle, the platonic 'idea'; or all three may be seen as reciprocal expressions of one meaning on different levels" (4:xv). And, as René Guénon pointedly observes, "There is indeed over-eager acceptance of the belief that to allow a symbolic meaning [to an event] must imply the rejection of the literal or historical meaning" (qtd. in 4:xiv). Could it be that many are eager to accept the "symbolic" and "spiritualized" aspects of Christianity because the plain idea of God becoming flesh is still as scandalous as ever, still an open rebuke to our spiritual pride? Surely, we say, we do not need a God to become human for us! And even if God did so, is it possible that humans as innately good as we are would crucify Him? Surely these stories are myths only, not objectively factual accounts—so our pride might want to insist.

The Union of Myth and History

We might summarize: To allow a mythic or symbolic meaning to a story does not imply that we cannot also allow for its literal or historical meaning. Following this vein of thought, W. Norman Pittenger disagrees explicitly with John Knox and implicitly with the Campbellian / sociological view. "The word 'myth' does not seem to me to be a satisfactory term to use to describe such events as the Incarnation of God in Christ or the Atonement wrought by him," he writes in *The Word Incarnate*:

> It is of the nature of "myth" to be descriptive either of ultimate and unique "events," such as the creation of the world or the end of history; or of universal and general truths. . . .
>
> However, the Incarnation of God in Christ and the Atonement wrought by him are in a different category. When we speak of these, we are not talking about things which like the creation and the consummation are "before" or "after" history. Nor are we talking about universal truths. . . . The stories of the Incarnation and the Atonement are tied up with a specific historical event; they have their grounding in something that actually happened in the course of human history. . . .
>
> It seems to me quite misleading to put the life of Christ in the same category as the "myth" of creation. . . ., as nothing more than types or helpful representations of what is universally true of human experience in relationship to God. . . . It is for these reasons that I should wish to speak of the life of Christ, with all its consequences in history, as the saga or story of God's supreme and definitive action. (11:39-41)

Knox, in response, merely maintains, "I should say we must regard them all as either 'myths' or 'stories' or both; and that the fact that one of them stands in a different relation to what we call history than the others, while it makes a difference, does not make so much difference—or better perhaps, does not make a difference of such kind—as to require the use of a separate category" (5:54-55). This is somewhat puzzling; Knox addresses the central objection to his stance by a simple contradiction. He carries the point a little further later by saying that when speaking of an event such as, for example, the Redemption, "the fact that it utilizes certain data which are historical— that is, some of the facts of Jesus' career—does not make it so" (5:62).

In this statement, Knox seems to overlook the fact that Pittenger is not saying the events of Christ's life are *solely* historical. Not only does Pittenger claim that the events of Christ's life are "specific" to "human history," but also and simultaneously that they make up a "saga or story"; these simultaneous claims do seem to require a "separate category" in that these claims could not be made in parallel cases such as the story of Prometheus's "crucifixion" or Osiris's "resurrection." Osiris is certainly story material, but he is not also specific to human history. The mythos of Christ, though similar in many respects to these myths, is also, and equally importantly to the Christian, fixed in historical data by eye-witnesses of that data.

As he progresses in his argument, Knox admits that "myth does . . . make contact with actual fact," but goes on to say that this "actual fact" is "experienced" fact, "not scientific or historical fact" (5:73). This strikes me as quibbling at best (what historical fact is not "experienced" by its participants?); at worst, it is missing the point of the dialectic, in the religious view, between myth and history, the dialectic of the "truthful lie." Again, Niebuhr expresses this difficult proposition well:

> What is true in the Christian religion can be expressed only in symbols which contain a certain degree of provisional and superficial deception. We do teach the truth by deception. . . . The necessity for the deception is given in the primary characteristic of the Christian world view. Christianity does not believe that the natural, temporal, and historical world is self-derived or self-explanatory. . . . The relation between the temporal and the eternal is dialectical. (1:3-4)

Similarly, Emil Brunner states both that "the certainty of faith lies on another plane than the secular certainty of historical facts" (12:25) and that Christianity's connection "with a historical event and person" is "indispensable" (12:14). Both propositions are affirmed.

A comparison may be of benefit here. The "In the beginning was the Word" of John 1:1 is much like the "In the beginning God created" of Genesis 1:1, in that both statements have meaning only in reference to or by virtue of the story (myth) in which they are found; both therefore lie outside of chronological history. Both may be said to correspond roughly to the "Once upon a time" of fairy tales (which, of course, elevates the status of "fairy tales" considerably, while not denigrating in the slightest the status of sacred literature). This is why attempts on the part of some religious persons to fix a historical date for Genesis 1:1 seem to be inevitably frustrated, for the only possible date is that given: "In the beginning."

In the case of John 1:1, however, an important and qualitative change takes place, for here the Word (myth) which exists "in the beginning" is also said to become a part of chronological history, i.e., become "flesh." In answer to the query of Lévi-Strauss, "The problem is: where does mythology end and where does history start?" (13:38), Christianity claims that myth and history become concurrent; God's supreme action finds itself in a historical Person.

"The Gospels contain a fairy-story, or a story of a larger kind which embraces all the essence of fairy-stories," writes J.R.R. Tolkien. ". . . . But this story has entered History and the primary world; the desire and aspiration of sub-creation [mythic artistry] has been raised to the fulfillment of Creation [the realm of historical experience]" (14:71-72).

Time Both Linear and Repetitive

Some leading mythologists concede on this point what Campbell and Knox deny; for instance, Mircea Eliade notes the dual relationship of the Christian to time, that though the "myth of eternal repetition . . . in the end made its way into Christian philosophy," still we must remind ourselves that "for Christianity, time is real because it has a meaning—the Redemption" (15:143). Eliade knows well both the tragedy and the glory of the idea of historical revelation; today's human, "the man who has left the horizon of archetypes and repetition," can no longer defend himself against "the terror of history" except "through the idea of God" (15:161-62). Modern man is "irremediably identified with history and progress . . ., both implying the final abandonment of the paradise of archetypes and repetition" (15:162). (I might qualify this by saying "the final abandonment of archetypes and repetition as the *sole measure* of history and as the *sole gauge* of truth." Today's "historicists" seem to fall into the equal and opposite error of making "truth" solely equivalent to the swarm of historical events—and since these are, in any case, no longer capturable, neither, to the historicists, is "truth.")

Eliade himself makes a similar qualification elsewhere; he says that, though "Christianity has nothing to fear" from pre-Christian mythoi because "its specificity is . . . guaranteed by *faith* as the category *sui generis* of religious experience, and by its valorization in *history*" (16:29, emphasis in original), still there is a sense in which "Christianity is prolonging a 'mythical' conduct of life into the modern world" (16:31). Exactly so; and this sense lies in religion's "rejection of profane time and the periodical recovery of the Great Time" (16:30), or the Christian Testament's distinction between *chronos* (our time-oriented reality) and "eternal life," not as a future event but as a present reality to its possessor, established as archetype or repetition by the

Liturgy, or even by the simplest Christian church meeting. The Christian lives in history (like Christ), but also as part of the eternal myth outside of time (also like Christ).

Therefore, in view of this dual concept of time, the religious person, whatever his or her historical context, "always believes that there is an absolute reality, *the sacred*, which transcends this world but manifests itself in this world, thereby sanctifying it and making it real" (17:202). This religious person further believes, according to Eliade:

> . . . the two points of view [symbolic and historical] are only superficially irreconcilable . . ., for it must not be thought that a symbolic connotation annuls the material and specific validity of an object or action. Symbolism *adds* a new value to an object or an act, without thereby violating its immediate or "historical" validity. (qtd. in 4:xiv)

Finally, this religious person believes that "human existence" only "participates in reality" in proportion as that existence is "religious" (17:202).

So this "idea of God" by which the religious person staves off "the terror of history" becomes of primary importance. The Christian has hope for the future even in the face of the dreadful and inevitable passage of time, for time itself is seen as both linear (historical) and eternally repetitive (mythic). This dual view of time, as well as this hope for the future, is found for the Christian in Christ, the manifested apex of both myth and history.

Chapter 4

A Christian Response to Myth

We now find ourselves in position to make two statements regarding the paradoxical approach to myth which I consider the most meaningful Christian response: (1) We may say that the Christian insists upon both the archetypal or symbolic aspect *and the particularity* of Christ. Neither aspect is to be neglected in favor of the other. (2) Concomitantly with this, we may also say that the Christian insists upon the view of time and history as *both cyclical and linear*, the eternal life of God being manifested within our time-locked condition.

The Circle and the Cross

Both of these conceptions can be seen even in some well-known and widely accepted Christian symbolism, such as the Celtic and Oxford crosses (among many others), in which the familiar cross is found within a circle. Here, as in some Eastern symbols, the circle represents recurrence, repetition, the cyclical mythic renewals in which we find "eternity." However, the symbol does not end with the circle, for centrally placed we find the cross, an intersection of two straight lines at a central point, that central point being a specific moment in history when eternal life became a part of linear time and dwelt among us.

"The great Asiatic symbol of a serpent with its tail in its mouth is really a very perfect image of a certain idea of unity and recurrence," writes Chesterton. ". . . . It really is a curve that in one sense includes everything, and in another sense comes to nothing" (1:266). He goes on to say:

> The cross has become something more than a historical memory; it does convey, almost as by a mathematical diagram, the truth about the real point at issue; the idea of a conflict stretching outwards into eternity. . . . In other words the cross, in fact as well as figure, does really stand for the idea of breaking out of the circle that is everything and nothing. . . . Christianity does appeal to a solid truth outside itself; to something which is in that sense external as well as eternal. (1:266-67)

So, in the Christian view, the vitalizing and life-renewing powers of archetype and repetition become encapsulated or summarized in the conception of divine personality, or personage. Nature (or flesh, in the Christian view) is sanctified without ceasing to be natural; the myth becomes history without ceasing to be myth. "The Word became flesh, and dwelt among us." The religious believer clings to this paradox as the means to an "understanding" which transcends understanding.

The Transcendent Mythic Order

But this "understanding" on the part of the religious believer is the perception granted by *vision*, for the ultimate irrationality cannot, of course, be apprehended by rationality, but only by the paradoxical dialectic; it seems incapable of systematic articulation without, as Aquinas puts it, a great admixture of error on the part of the articulator (*S.T.* I.i.i). Nevertheless, the dialectic of faith exists. "All those contradictions," as Pascal writes, "which seemed to take me furthest from the knowledge of any religion are what led me most directly to the true" (2:146).

Religious faith, then, becomes not reason's goal, but its necessary condition. How else to reason without the fundamental and primary element of an all-embracing *vision* or perception? How else might we relate to the paradox which is ourselves?—not by reasoning it out, but by *seeing* it. How else might we understand ourselves as flesh and spirit, sacred and profane? How else to understand the nature of the universe in which we find ourselves placed? Most importantly, how else to regard Christ, the "only-begotten" of the Father who has now become the "first-born among many brethren"?

In keeping with the cyclical nature of myth, we might conclude this little study by returning to the poet with whom we began. A few lines from Wallace Stevens's poem, "The Connoisseur of Chaos," seem appropriate:

A. A violent order is disorder; and
B. A great disorder is an order. These
Two things are one . . . (3:215)

When faced with the order of the "useful lies" of mythic art and the apparent disorder of "reality," including the ultimate realities with which both mythic art and religion insist they deal, the religious believer has reason for perplexity. But the paradox of the Incarnation, the paradox of the immersion of mythic order into the flux of historical reality, at least leaves the door open intellectually to the idea of religious truth, the idea of a redemptive mythic order which transcends the merely sociological or psychological view of myth espoused in many "myth studies" today, a redemptive mythic order which arises out of *actual spiritual experience.* (The reader may be interested to know that before his death Wallace Stevens joined the Catholic Church. We may therefore hope that, in Christ, Stevens found the union of myth, artistic order, and historical substance which he in his poetry questioned and sought.)

The historian and the mythic artist are not finally one and the same. In the person of the believer, however, they may reach the same conclusions and find themselves on the same side: the side of redemption, the side of faith, the side of truth. As the Trinity is One, so also the Christ of history and of myth is One; the ideals of historical truth and of the symbolic, aesthetic truth known to the myth-maker finally merge, blend, become a single coherent vision, to the eye of faith.

Appendix

The Interaction of Experience and Language

Henri Bergson expresses some interesting criticisms of Zeno's "arrow" paradox. This paradox is designed to show that motion or change is impossible; that is, because an arrow in flight is always at rest exactly where it is at every moment and cannot be anywhere else at that moment, there is no possibility of change in the arrow when considered moment by moment, for it is always at rest, and hence there is also no possibility of motion. However, Bergson maintains that Zeno's whole premise is wrong—that the arrow can never *be at rest* because it is always in the process of *becoming*. Even when it (or anything else, for that matter) appears to be at rest, it is nonetheless always fluid at least in the dimension of time. So, since all things exist in space and time, all things are also always sometime and someplace other than where they are *now*, since where they are *now* no longer exists; that time and place have passed by, even in the time taken to read this sentence.

If the reader is still with me, the simple conclusion to all this may already have been anticipated: Since physical experiences themselves are so fluid in definition, is it surprising that the language used to describe them is equally evasive and slippery? Is this not especially true when the language used is metaphorical in nature, as in most mythic and religious language?

The Independent Existence of Experience and Language

In the face of this question, however, my thesis is that language at least moves with our experience of reality, and that experience and language therefore have a non-independent relationship between them which at least implies the *independent* existence of both. This also implies a commitment both to ontological and semantic realism, both of which will be defined shortly. This relationship between reality and language can be seen both in the nature of our daily experience and in the nature of our use of language.

A familiar story from Boswell describes how he and Dr. Johnson were discussing Berkeley's philosophical theories. At length, Boswell remarked that, although he found Berkeley's theories clearly false, he also found them impossible to refute. Upon hearing this, the ever-practical Johnson soundly kicked a large stone, saying as he did so, "I refute it *thus*."

Most people may be broadly classified into three types in their reactions to this story: (1) There are non-philosophical types who think that Johnson's action quite adequately proves what Johnson sets out to prove. (2) There are contrary types who think that Johnson by his action proves absolutely nothing. (3) Finally, there are other types who also think that Johnson by his action proves absolutely nothing, but who sympathize with the effort, since they themselves have often felt like kicking a few rocks during the course of philosophical discussions. How is it, exactly, that one proves not only the actual, mind-independent existence of reality, but also the "literalness" of our language about reality? If even physical objects such as boulders present problems as one attempts to answer these questions, how much more aspects of reality that are not physical (God's existence, for example). Is God merely a "metaphor," as Joseph Campbell flatly declares? Or, when we refer to God, are we referring to a reality that exists independently of our own imaginative, mind-bound creation?

The general position that answers "Yes" to this last question I am going to call "realism," both metaphysical and semantic, throughout this appendix.

Definitions and Problems of Realism

In his forthcoming work *Truth and Correspondence*, Richard Fumerton of the University of Iowa points out, probably correctly, that "when we try to be precise . . . about what a metaphysical realist's commitments are, the matter becomes extremely vague very quickly" (1:1.14). However, at that risk, I would like to both highlight and attempt to defend some of those commitments. For example, David L. Anderson, in an article discussing philosopher Hilary Putnam's "internal realism," defines realism as "a conjunction of commitments— ontological, semantic, and alethic" (2:51). In order to call oneself a realist, he maintains, one must adhere to three fundamental "metaphysical tenets of realism":

> . . . *Correspondence Truth.* Truth is a relation of correspondence between pieces of language and the world (i.e., *ding-an-sich* reality).
> . . .
> *Semantic Realism.* Statements that express an existential commitment to concrete objects . . . will be true or false in virtue of the intrinsic nature of mind-independent reality, and thus in virtue of conditions the obtaining of which may be, in principle, inaccessible to human beings.
> *Ontological Realism.* All (or most) of the objects . . . countenanced by twentieth-century science and common sense exist independently of any mind. (2:51)

Putnam, in one place or another, has rejected all of these tenets in favor of an "internal realism" which smacks rather of the tradition of Kantian idealism. For example, to most metaphysical realists, the "truth" of a proposition would be non-epistemic in nature, i.e., the proposition would simply bear the relation of correspondence to a mind-independent reality. However, Putnam in his 1976 Presidential Address to the American Philosophical Association, agreed with Michael Dummett that this picture of truth is unfeasible:

> The point is that Dummett and I agree that you can't treat understanding a sentence (in general) as knowing its truth conditions. . . . We both agree that the theory of understanding has to be done in a verificationist way. . . . But now . . . I have given Dummett all he needs to demolish metaphysical realism—a picture I was wedded to! (3:129)

We can perhaps deal with some of Putnam's objections to metaphysical realism shortly. For example, in his *Reason, Truth, and History* (1981), he proposes his own "commitments" to which, he says, metaphysical realism must adhere. The second of these commitments is the view that "there is exactly one true and complete description of 'the way the world is' " (4:49). Notice, however, Anderson's own conjunction of commitments, listed above, in which he maintains that "the intrinsic nature of mind-independent reality" is simply what it is in itself, even though it may be outside the range of "one true and complete description" of it. And Fumerton goes so far as to say that the moderate realist (one who is committed to the mind-independence of the world except for those aspects of the world that are trivially mind-dependent, such as thoughts) could even "embrace with open arms the idea that there is such a thing as conceptual relativity" (1:1.10; see also 1.9 ff.).

In fact, so staunch a realist as Aquinas pointed out several hundred years ago that most language is not "univocal" with experience (i.e., corresponding with reality in only one way, or in an exact, one-to-one relationship). On the other hand, neither is language "equivocal" with experience (that is, having no relationship to reality at all, or else a completely arbitrary relationship). Rather, Thomas describes much language as *analogical* in nature, and therefore linked to experience in a relationship that is perhaps arbitrary in particulars, but necessary in overall concept. In this view, language at least *moves with* experience, the link between the two being a correspondence relationship of cause (reality) and effect (the language used to describe reality). In other words, experience does not provoke a *necessary language*, a language necessary in itself in every particular, but experience does provoke the *effect of language*, or semantic representation. This representation is not the "one true and complete description" of the world, as Putnam says realists must have. In Thomist terms, it is not a "univocal" description. However, neither is it "equivocal"; it is "analogical," and as such implies a mind-independent reality from which the mind-dependent analogies of language are made.

A non-realist such as philosopher Nelson Goodman (or "irrealist," to use Goodman's own term) might eradicate the problem of semantic reference to the mind-independent world by denying that such reference could exist, and by asserting that all semantics must be understood in terms of "frames of reference" and not in terms of relation to a mind-independent world: "Frames of reference . . . belong less to what is described than to systems of description" (5:2). In this description of reference and meaning in language, "We are not speaking in terms of multiple possible alternatives to a single actual world but of multiple actual worlds" (5:2). Goodman goes on to say:

> If I ask about the world, you can offer to tell me how it is under one or more frames of reference; but if I insist that you tell me how it is apart from all frames, what can you say? We are confined to ways of describing whatever is described. Our universe, so to speak, consists of these ways rather than of a world or worlds. (5:2-3)

This statement appears to contradict the idea of "multiple *actual* worlds" (emphasis added), since it speaks only of "ways of describing" rather than of "actual" worlds. However, the central "irrealist" point still remains: that we cannot understand or know what the world is in itself, or even know the world at all, apart from an action of the orchestrating mind, the imposition of a "frame of reference."

Of course, this idea, if true, would prove devastating for any attempt at semantic realism (and several other types of realism, for that matter). As Putnam puts it, "The assumed correspondence between the representations in the speaker's mind and their external referents" is an important part of the realist model of reference (3:4). If this correspondence is undermined—if "reference" can be shown to be unfixed and therefore of necessity open to any "interpretation" or "conceptualization"—then metaphysical realism itself may well collapse.

The Cause / Effect Link

However, let me illustrate the link between the two (language and experienced reality), which I have earlier called a cause / effect relationship. Suppose a furry four-legged creature with a long tail—a cat—walks into the room. Whether we call this creature a cat, a *chat*, or *el gato*, the experience of the cat does provoke (or "cause") the effect of language to describe or designate it. No particular word in itself is necessary (as witness the fact that the same creature is designated differently in different languages), but the effect of language, the linguistic representation of experience, is provoked by the same occasion, the feline appearance. Likewise, for another example, even though our description of the universe is much different today than Ptolemy's was yesterday, those causal factors that prompted Ptolemy's descriptions of the universe are exactly the same as those causal factors that prompt our descriptions of the universe, these causal factors being independent of the differing use of terms within differing traditions of knowledge. Since both Ptolemy's term "universe" and our term "universe" indicate relationships that are causally connected, we can say that they "genuinely refer" to the same entity. As a semantic realist might say, these theoretical terms correspond to the real structural features of the world.

The objection might be raised at this point, however, that, since language does modify experience, experienced reality in fact is *not* independent. However, no matter what we choose to designate by our language, no matter where our semantic representations intersect with experience, the experience itself continues and is susceptible to designation by language through someone else's perception of it. If an experience is susceptible to semantic representation, it does not really matter that our own interaction with and representation of that experience is fragmentary, or even *necessarily* fragmentary. This fragmentary interaction and representation does not change the independent character of that which is knowable, or that which is susceptible to representation.

I am assuming, of course, that in order to be "a metaphysical realist about the external world," then one should also be a "semantic realist about all external-world statements," as Anderson has it (6:1). Can one find a way to hold to the mind-independence of the external world as well as the idea that truth or falsity in semantics resides in a proposition's correspondence or non-correspondence to that mind-independent world?

"Direct Realism": A Form of Semi-Thomism?

Putnam's definition of conceptual relativity revolves around the claim that "the logical primitives themselves, and in particular the notions of object and existence, have a multitude of different uses rather than one absolute 'meaning' " (7:19). If a slight digression may be permitted in an already long appendix, I think Panayot Butchvarov's discussion of the special character of "existence" presents ideas that are valuable not only for the sake of Butchvarov's own variety of realism ("direct" realism), but for a better understanding of the thought of metaphysical realism as well.

In "Our Robust Sense of Reality," after a presentation of the concept of "non-existent objects," Butchvarov asks:

But what explains the power of the conviction that all objects exist? Why do most philosophers share it, if it is so plainly wrong? The reason, I suggest, is the special character of the concept of existence. (8:411)

To Butchvarov, the concept of "existence" is a "transcendental concept," i.e., it has classificatory application, but does not stand for anything: "Although we do have this concept and it is genuinely classificatory, i.e., it applies to some objects and not to others, it is not a concept that stands for anything, real or unreal, individual or a property or a relation" (8:412). At first it may seem odd to think of "existence" as not standing for anything "real," since to many or even most people, "existence" would seem to be the most basic property of all real objects. However, Butchvarov points out that in this he is in fundamental agreement with "Aristotle and the medieval philosophers who accepted the doctrine of the transcendentals . . . because they held that being is not a genus, that the concept of being . . . corresponded to nothing that all beings share" (9:56).

In this, I think, we find the "semi-Thomism" to which I refer in the subtitle of this section. Aquinas writes that "being is the first thing that comes into the intellect" (*Met.* I.2.46). This intellectual attainment comes about "by simple apprehension . . . which is analytically prior to judgment" (10:181). The simple fact of being comes before any other thinking processes take place. Butchvarov also seems to think that the concept of material being is primary, and that all forms of subsequent predication are to be understood in terms of it (see, for example, his *Being Qua Being*, 1979). Again, this seems similar to Thomist thought. As Ralph McInerny, a leading Thomist, states, paraphrasing Aquinas, "It is the quiddity of material things which is the connatural object of the human intellect" (10:182).

The concepts or ideas formed by the mind are ways of knowing sensory data first of all, before any judgments can be made regarding the essential or accidental qualities of the material things revealed in sensory data: "At the outset of the intellectual life, there will be no question of forming a concept which will be applied to anything other than what is attained by the senses" (10:182). Even this does not signify the concept of "existence," for "being" merely signifies "nothing other than what is," not that "something exists" (10:184). Even the concept of existence itself does not necessarily signify "something exists," which would be a sort of existential judgment regarding being. If existence were not conceived directly through the impact of material identity, no existential judgment regarding that material identity (including the judgment "something exists") would be possible. So the existentialist formula "Existence precedes essence" is wrong, according to this view; the essence of existence (material being) actually precedes existence, if we conceive of existence as a series of judgments regarding that-which-is (being).

However, two crucial differences between Aquinas and Butchvarov also begin to emerge here, for Aquinas (1) allows for the perceiving "I" or self in his description of the perception of material objects, and (2) allows for a formally causal relationship between reality and our consciousness of it. To Aquinas, it is not true that "our intellectual faculties know only the impression made on them," for "the intellect [also] reflects upon itself [and] by such reflection it understands both its own act of intelligence, and the species by which it understands" (*S.T.* I.85.2). So Aquinas describes "the thing actually understood" thus: "In these words 'the thing actually understood,' there is a double implication: the thing which is understood, and the fact that it is understood" (*S.T.* I.85.2). The "thing which is understood" is that-which-is (being); the "concept" or "idea" is that-by-which we understand. "The thing actually understood" implies both (11:128 ff.).

The "consciousness" of reality is the "idea" of its being. Predication or semantic representation, on the one hand, is a purely *logical* relation; it does not pertain to the consciousness of reality, but rather pertains to our mode of apprehending separately what exists as a unity in that consciousness. On the other hand, the relation between reality and our consciousness of it does seem to be a relation of formal causality. Things are called real because they are the causes of the consciousness of reality in the intellect; this consciousness compares to reality as an effect to a cause (*Met.* V.9.896). This causal relation is explicitly denied by Butchvarov, although he does allow for the logical relation:

> The so-called "intuition" behind the causal theory is that the object
> perceived is somehow necessary for the occurrence of the perceiving.
> But direct realism acknowledges this: the object, even if not real, is a
> logically necessary element of the perceiving. (12:3)

Despite this denial, Butchvarov's ideas, out of all those covered thus far, seem closest to a metaphysical and semantic realist conception. Certainly his discussion of "existence" helps greatly to clarify matters in discussion of what it means for something to be "real" and for something to "exist."

A Short Defense of Metaphysical Realism

The temptation at this point is always present for the metaphysical realist simply to step back from the debate by rejecting all non-realist premises: "The non-realist says we could possibly be brains in vats [Putnam], or perhaps deceived by an evil supernatural creature

[Descartes]? Well, I say we could not possibly be so constituted or so deceived—at least not to the level of fine-tuned complexity these possibilities would require—and therefore all conclusions derived from these premises are simply false." Isn't realism about as obvious as any philosophical doctrine could be? However, to give in completely to this temptation would not only be unfair to the other participants in the debate, but also to those millions of sincere Hindu and Buddhist believers who are, at some level or another, non-realists in the philosophical commitments underlying their religious beliefs. To them, whether or not realism is an "obvious" doctrine has little or nothing to do with whether or not it is true.

Therefore (assuming that the arguments adduced so far against other forms of realism and non-realism are both valid and correct), I will advance my short defense of metaphysical and semantic realism (and conclude this appendix) simply by making three observations. In making these observations, I am going to reject explicitly only one anti-realist assumption, albeit admittedly a major one:

Observation # 1: Thomas Nagel brings up the point that metaphysical realism is a *precondition* for some of our statements and beliefs if we believe at all in causal relations, since certain objects of reference (such as the aforementioned causal relations) cannot be described with great success without a theoretical metaphysical foundation. As Nagel puts it, if a person who denies metaphysical realism cannot sensibly account for causality, and the metaphysical realist can, the better account seems obvious (13:30).

So the logical follow-up questions would be left hanging here: Just how successful is metaphysical realism at accounting for causal relations? Are causal links implausible (at best), or impossible to discover even if they do exist (at worst)? Considering how difficult it is to account plausibly for causal relations, appealing to metaphysical realism as the "better" or "best" account of them seems problematic. Nevertheless, that is exactly what I would like to do, in agreement with Nagel.

In the standard format for causal arguments, one or more of the following hold:

1. A causes B in P.
2. B causes A in P.
3. Some third factor independently causes both A and B in P, and neither situation 1 nor 2 holds.
4. There is no causal connection between A and B in P, and any correlation is accidental. (14:311)

These are the only alternatives in a causal argument. Although they are not all mutually exclusive, if three alternatives can be eliminated from consideration, the fourth must hold. Therefore, let us consider a causal chain of events, such as this one: Turning the water taps in my kitchen sink (action A) leads to water flowing from the spigot (result B). Situation 2 does not seem to hold, since it has never been the case that the flow of water preceded the turning of the taps. Inductively, situations 3 or 4 have never been the case in my experience; to believe either of them to be true would require a leap of faith immeasurably greater than the simple acceptance of situation 1 (A causes B in P) as the true account. Of course, this argument is inductive in nature, and does not lead to a logically air-tight deductive conclusion. Therefore, to accept situation 1 as the true account of the occurrence entails also an acceptance of the theoretical metaphysical foundation, i.e., an acceptance of causal relations between A (the cause) and B (the effect). This also has obvious implications for a metaphysical causal account of perception, the reality of the external world being the cause of the effect of perceptions, and eventually the cause of our semantic representations of it as well.

Observation # 2: The second observation I would like to make follows from the first, and revolves around the semantic / linguistic claims of semantic realism. A pillar of anti-realist arguments seems to be the idea that attempts to depict or define "truth" are already encased in language, and that therefore reference cannot simply correspond to ontologically independent states of affairs, but must always refer only to other mind-dependent / linguistic entities. Certainly, to the non-realist, reference cannot simply correspond to a *single* ontologically independent state of affairs.

My short response is that, again, metaphysical realism would seem to be a precondition for semantics, which by its nature seems to presuppose a metaphysical (i.e., non-epistemic) reality beyond language and beyond cognition, a reality that serves as the causal agent for our terms of language. The denial of this non-epistemic reality involves one in a "vicious regress," as Fumerton has pointed out:

> One observation we might make about the anti-realists's rhetoric is that there tends to be very little talk about the ontological status of representations or concepts. When we are told that because "the elements of what we call 'language' or 'mind' penetrate so deeply into what we call 'reality' " it is a mistake to suppose that there is some reality that exists independently of the contributions of mind, we are surely left wondering what it is that is making all these contributions,

doing all this "world making." Do representations or concepts exist independently of *their* representations, or are they "made" the same way everything else is supposed to be made? And if they are, what makes them, and the makers of them, and the makers of them, and so on ad infinitum. (1:4.2)

Intentionality alone certainly cannot serve as this causal agent; as Butchvarov (himself certainly a believer in the intentional nature of consciousness) writes, "We must have direct access to *something* that is unconceptualized if we are to conceptualize it" (12:12). We are initially and primarily acquainted with the unconceptualized fact of the causal agent, that is, the fact of the world: "[T]here is no reason to suppose that we are never acquainted with unconceptualized facts," as Fumerton maintains (1:3.13).

Therefore, whatever this causal agent "really" is—and *despite whether or not we can ever even know what it "really" is* (15:225)—we can know that "it is neither identical with the language we use to describe it, nor is it the product in any ultimate sense of our thoughts about it" (16:5). This causal agent must be ultimately described as ontologically independent, and "truth and falsehood must in the end yield to this immovable force" (1:1.11).

Observation # 3: My third observation follows from the first two, and in this one I finally must simply deny one of the foundational premises of the anti-realist. I deny that the existence of the external world is a postulate that requires demonstration. That is, I deny that the causal agent described in Observations #1 and #2 *needs* demonstration, for its existence is self-evident. As Etienne Gilson writes:

> This conviction of the reliability of our senses is simply the self-evidence of our experience. Since we are here concerned with self-evidence, it is futile to demand a demonstration. All we can do for one who does not see something is point it out to him. If he then sees it, well and good, but we cannot begin to prove to him that he does see it. The difficulties begin only when the philosopher undertakes to transform this sensible certitude into a demonstrative certitude of the intellect. (17:181)

In fact, in making existential judgments regarding being, or that-which-is, or that-which-is-understood, does not the perceiving subject typically treat the sensible world as the mathematician treats a non-demonstrable axiom? Would we ask a mathematician to demonstrate such an axiom—$A = A$, for instance? Isn't our requirement of the metaphysical realist to demonstrate the reality of the sensible world and its causal relation to truthful propositions such a mistake?

Now, it is certainly true that we can and do separate the sensible world from the conceptual world. However, this seems to me to be only a *logical* separation, not a separation in reality, as when, for instance, we separate the concept of "wetness" from the sensible experience of liquid-state "water." It is true that water and wetness are conceptually not the same, but it is also true that water cannot sensibly be separated from wetness in reality. It is true that the concept of a table's existence (for example) goes beyond the sensible experience of the table; but it is also true that the sensible experience of the table entails its existence; i.e., the sensible experience is just as much a true form of knowledge as the conceptual.

Another sentence from Gilson summarizes this observation neatly: "In order to understand the realist position and accept it in its purity [he is, I think, referring to metaphysical realism], it is necessary to recall that, in the order of existential judgments, *sensible perception has the nature and value of a principle of knowledge*" (17:183, emphasis added). As Descartes did *not* say: *Sum; ergo, cogito.* I am, for I find myself in existence in a sensible world; therefore, I am able to think and make assertions about that world. The degree to which these thoughts and assertions are true depends upon the degree to which they correspond to the sensible world which is their primary cause.

However, it is only fair to say that this version of metaphysical and semantic realism is not terribly popular today. Contemporary philosopher Richard Rorty, for one, mocks this notion. In twentieth-century philosophy, the focus of attention has shifted from the relationship between reality, the senses, and correspondence, to the relationship between purely linguistic constructs. The world is based on "contingency," Rorty says, and to say that the world of experience has any sort of intrinsic, ongoing nature is "a remnant of the idea that the world is a divine creation, the work of someone who had something in mind, who Himself spoke some language in which He described His own project" (qtd. in 18:478).

The Primal Language

In my view, however, it is at least curious that this idea of the world as based on language is more or less universal; for example, even apart from the Greek, Hebrew, and Christian traditions, many Native American accounts describe the universe as beginning with a "shout." Some Eastern religions have similar beliefs:

> . . . Hindu mythology maintains that everything was called into being
> by *Vak*, which is speech, or *shabda*, sound. Indeed, the Hindus insist
> that the roots of their sacred language, Sanskrit, are not merely the
> roots of verbs and nouns, but the roots of things themselves, which
> come into being by the utterance of the primordial words. (19:69)

It is also curious that the "remnant" of this idea (a world based on
language) still stubbornly survives to this day; one would have thought
that thousands of years of experience with language would have
revealed to us its true nature by now (unless, of course, the true nature
of language *has* already revealed itself to us, in just this form I am
attempting to describe, and which Rorty mocks).

In the early thought of Ludwig Wittgenstein, in his *Tractatus
Logico-Philosophicus*, the necessity for this primary language is
recognized. Semantic representation, he felt, must possess the inner
logic first possessed by that which is represented. Rutgers professor
Colin McGinn paraphrases Wittgenstein as saying,

> Language and the world are one, in their deep metaphysical essence.
> . . . There must exist an ideal language in which the necessary
> sameness of form with reality is made fully transparent. To construct
> such a language would be to devise a symbolic system in which the
> structure of the world would reach right through our modes of
> representation: a flawless metaphysical mirror, as it were. (20:34-35)

What is it in humans which drives us to seek the reality unmediated by
symbol, the "word" and "flesh" united as one, that place where "myth"
and "history" meet and merge?

The great teacher and rhetorician Richard Weaver writes, "At the
beginning I should urge examining in all seriousness that ancient belief
that a divine element is present in language. . . . A man can bind
himself in the face of contingencies by saying Yea or Nay, which can
only mean that words in common human practice express something
transcending the moment" (21:148). The modern temper, Rorty's
words being a good example, would regard this notion as outdated or
archaic. However, just because an idea is *old* does not necessarily
mean it is *outdated.* It very well may be old because it is true; and this
older view at least has the added benefit of explaining the continuity of
that experience which is not linguistically described or even perceived.

For example, the Greek verb *poiéo*, from whence we derive our
word for "poem" or "poetry," is defined as "to make, form, construct,
or (when used of God) create." This view of the relationship between
language and creation holds that underneath the continuity of the
experience we perceive and describe runs a primal creative Word, in
which there is no distinction between the designation and that which is

designated, no mediating symbol for the reality. All of existence, if you will, becomes a *poem*. Christianity, for example, describes the pre-existent Christ as "the Word Incarnate"; what I am saying is that *all* of our experience can be seen as the "incarnation" of primal language, the existential phenomenon which fulfills the mythic metaphor. Our own linguistic designations of experience would then be seen as derived from the original, primal, ongoing linguistic designation which is identical with experience.

To be "truthful" or "accurate" in language would then simply be to correspond in semantic representation more and more closely to the ongoing reality of that which is represented.

The Interaction of Experience and Language

Allow me to repeat this point: Our present-day use of language can be seen as being derived from the primal semantic representation which is itself identical with our present-day experience; or, as the classical Greeks, the ancient Hebrews, and the early Christians all believed (in different forms), the physical world is ordered and upheld by the *Logos*-principle, "upholding all things by the word of his power" (Hebrews 1:3). Our own language then could be seen as not being identical with experience or primal language, but as deriving its character from it, like a photograph deriving its image from the reality before the camera. And because of this, even those aspects of our experience which "cannot be put into words" can still be apprehended, or seen, despite the lack of a inner logical form which can be semantically represented. These aspects of our experience would still be knowable, for reality itself would not be necessarily restricted to the image of reality produced by our use of language. These are the aspects of our experience that are truly mythic, as opposed to sociological or psychological. This is what God may finally desire for us: that as Christ is myth become fact, so the experienced facts of our lives may become part of His eternally living Myth.

At any rate, we freely admit that language very often modifies experience as much as vice versa. To use the camera analogy once more: The very fact that a guiding intelligence has chosen to represent this portion of experience rather than that one changes the experience itself to a degree, since a fraction of the rush of experience becomes isolated as an image on film. However, my central point is that neither the image nor the reality therefore eliminates the other. "Out there" is still "out there"; and so, though language and experience have a non-independent link between them, this link implies as well the independent existence of both, as both the nature of our daily experience and the nature of our use of language to represent that daily experience indicate.

Therefore, the metaphors we use in religious language (contrary to Joseph Campbell's flat declaration, "God is a metaphor") are not identical with the reality they seek to describe. "How can we describe God? With what image [of our own devising] can we compare him?" (Isaiah 40:18). The analogical predications we make regarding any aspect of reality are not identical with the unitary meaning of the reality itself.

Our Task

Our task, then, becomes simple to understand, if not to accomplish: We must strive to ensure that (1) our language and (2) the reality provoking our language, to the best of our abilities, correspond. If I understand it correctly, this is the guiding purpose behind the study of semantics.

Moreover, if the word "knowledge" is substituted for the word "language" in the first sentence of the preceding paragraph, this also becomes the guiding purpose behind *all* of our intellectual activity: to ensure that our knowledge corresponds with reality. Therefore, and finally, our intellectual activity becomes moral activity as well. The lesser is subsumed in the greater.

References

All quotes from Thomas Aquinas are either from his *Commentary on the Metaphysics of Aristotle, Vol. I* (translated by John P. Rowan. Chicago: Henry Regnery Co., 1961), or his *Summa Theologica, Vol. I* (translated by the Fathers of the English Dominican Province, 1957). These are parenthetically documented as *Met.* and *S.T.*, respectively.

Introduction: Pictures in the Clouds

1. Wallace Stevens. *The Collected Poems.* New York: Random House, 1982.
2. Emil Brunner. *The Scandal of Christianity.* London: London Press, 1951.
3. Joe David Bellamy. *The New Fiction: Interviews with Innovative American Writers.* Chicago: Univ. of Illinois Press, 1974.
4. *Voices and Visions # 11: Wallace Stevens.* Videocassette. Prod. New York Center for Visual History. New York: The Annenberg / CPB Collection, 1988. 58 min.
5. C.S. Lewis. *Miracles: A Preliminary Study.* New York: Macmillan, 1947.

Chapter 1: Myth and the Central Questions

1. Eric Voegelin. *Conversations with Eric Voegelin.* Ed. R. Eric O'Connor. Montreal: Thomas More Institute, 1980.
2. Brunner. *The Scandal of Christianity.*

3.   David Bidney. "Myth, Symbolism, and Truth." *Myth: A Symposium.* Ed. Thomas A. Sebeok. Bloomington: Indiana Univ. Press, 1970. 3-24.

4.   Owen Jones. "Joseph Campbell and the Power of Myth." *The Intercollegiate Review* 25.1 (Fall 1989): 13-23.

5.   E.g., Robert A. Segal. "The Romantic Appeal of Joseph Campbell." *The Christian Century* 4 April 1990: 332-35.

6.   Joseph Campbell. *The Power of Myth.* Ed. Betty Sue Flowers. New York: Doubleday, 1988.

7.   Matthew Scully. "Adler v. Averroes." *National Review* 19 November 1990: 50-51.

8.   G.K. Chesterton. *The Everlasting Man. The Collected Works of G.K. Chesterton, Vol. II.* Ed. George J. Marlin, Richard P. Rabatin, and John L. Swan. San Francisco: Ignatius Press, 1986. 135-407.

9.   Joseph Campbell. *The Hero with a Thousand Faces.* Princeton, N.J.: Princeton Univ. Press, 1968.

10.   Mortimer Adler. "This Campbell Person." *National Review* 17 February 1992: 48-50.

11.   Mortimer Adler. *Truth in Religion: The Plurality of Religions and the Unity of Truth.* New York: Macmillan, 1990.

12.   Stephen Larsen and Robin Larsen. *A Fire in the Mind: The Life of Joseph Campbell.* New York: Doubleday, 1991.

Chapter 2: Should We Reject Myth Entirely?

1.   Ralph Earle. *Word Meanings in the New Testament.* Grand Rapids, Mich.: Baker Book House, 1989.

2.   Richardson, Alan. *Genesis I-XI. The Torch Bible Commentaries.* London: SCM Press, 1953.

3.   Ernest F. Scott. "The New Testament and Criticism." *The Abingdon Bible Commentary.* New York: Abingdon Press, 1929. 885-90.

4.   C.S. Lewis. "Myth Became Fact." *God in the Dock: Essays on Theology and Ethics.* Ed. Walter Hooper. Grand Rapids, Mich.: Eerdmans Publishing Co., 1970. 63-67.

5.   Susan V. Gallagher and Roger Lundin. *Literature through the Eyes of Faith.* New York: Harper & Row, 1989.

6.   Kenneth Wuest. *The Pastoral Epistles in the Greek New Testament. Word Studies in the Greek New Testament, Vol. II.* Grand Rapids, Mich.: Eerdmans Publishing Co., 1973.

Chapter 3: Myth and Religious Truth

1. Reinhold Niebuhr. *Beyond Tragedy: Essays on the Christian Interpretation of History.* New York: Scribner's, 1937.
2. Campbell. *The Hero with a Thousand Faces.*
3. Campbell. *The Power of Myth.*
4. J.E. Cirlot. *A Dictionary of Symbols.* Trans. Jack Sage. New York: Philosophical Library, 1962.
5. John Knox. *Myth and Truth: An Essay on the Language of Faith.* Charlottesville: Univ. Press of Virginia, 1964.
6. Rudolf Bultmann. *Jesus Christ and Mythology.* New York: Scribner's, 1958.
7. C.S. Lewis. *Surprised by Joy.* New York: Harcourt Brace Jovanovich, 1955.
8. Lewis. "Myth Became Fact."
9. Chesterton. *The Everlasting Man.*
10. Cornelius Loew. *Myth, Sacred History, and Philosophy.* New York: Harcourt, Brace, & World, 1967.
11. W. Norman Pittenger. *The Word Incarnate.* New York: Harper and Brothers, 1959.
12. Brunner. *The Scandal of Christianity.*
13. Claude Lévi-Strauss. *Myth and Meaning.* New York: Schocken Books, 1979.
14. J.R.R. Tolkien. "On Fairy-Stories." *Tree and Leaf.* London: George Allen & Unwin Ltd., 1964. 3-84.
15. Mircea Eliade. *The Myth of the Eternal Return, or, Cosmos and History.* Trans. Willard R. Trask. Princeton, N.J.: Princeton Univ. Press, 1974.
16. Mircea Eliade. *Myths, Dreams, and Mysteries: The Encounter between Contemporary Faiths and Archaic Realities.* Trans. Philip Mairet. New York: Harper & Row, 1960.
17. Mircea Eliade. *The Sacred and the Profane: The Nature of Religion.* Trans. Willard R. Trask. New York: Harcourt, Brace, & World, 1959.

Chapter 4: A Christian Response to Myth

1. Chesterton. *The Everlasting Man.*
2. Blaise Pascal. *Pensées.* Trans. A.J. Krailsheimer. New York: Penguin, 1988.
3. Stevens. *The Collected Poems.*

Appendix: The Interaction of Experience and Language

1. Richard Fumerton. *Truth and Correspondence.* As of this writing, this manuscript is under contract but unpublished. All quotes refer to the chapter numbers and page numbers within chapters of the actual manuscript, e.g., (1:2.9) is Chapter 2, page 9 of the manuscript.
2. David L. Anderson. "What Is Realistic about Putnam's Internal Realism?" *Philosophical Topics* 20.1 (Spring 1992): 49-83.
3. Hilary Putnam. *Meaning and the Moral Sciences.* London: Routledge & Kegan Paul, 1978.
4. Hilary Putnam. *Reason, Truth, and History.* Cambridge: Cambridge UP, 1981.
5. Nelson Goodman. *Ways of Worldmaking.* Indianapolis: Hackett Publishing Co., 1978.
6. David L. Anderson. "A Dogma of Metaphysical Realism." *American Philosophical Quarterly* 32.1 (Jan. 1995): 1-11.
7. Hilary Putnam. *The Many Faces of Realism.* LaSalle, Ill.: Open Court, 1987.
8. Panayot Butchvarov. "Our Robust Sense of Reality." *Grazer Philosophische Studien*: 403-21.
9. Panayot Butchvarov. "The Untruth and the Truth of Skepticism." *The Proceedings and Addresses of The American Philosophical Association* 67.4 (Jan. 1994): 41-61.
10. Ralph McInerny. *Being and Predication: Thomistic Interpretations.* Washington, D.C.: CUA Press, 1986. [For the "semi-Thomist" view, as I have labeled it, please see Panayot Butchvarov's *Being Qua Being: A Theory of Identity, Existence, and Predication.* Bloomington: Indiana UP, 1979.]
11. Peter Kreeft. *A Shorter Summa.* San Francisco: Ignatius Press, 1993.
12. Panayot Butchvarov. "Direct Realism without Materialism." *Midwest Studies in Philosophy* 19 (1994): 1-21.
13. Thomas Nagel. *The Last Word.* Oxford: Oxford UP, 1997.
14. Richard Feldman. *Reason and Argument.* 2nd ed. Upper Saddle River, N.J.: Prentice-Hall, 1999.
15. David Lewis. "Putnam's Paradox." *Australasian Journal of Philosophy* 62 (1984): 221-36.
16. Nick Meriweather. "On Being a Hip Metaphysical Realist." Proc. of a Conference on "Realism and Truth: 44th Annual Wheaton College Philosophy Conference." Wheaton, Illinois: Wheaton College. 23-25 October, 1997. Unpublished.
17. Etienne Gilson. *Thomist Realism and the Critique of Knowledge* (1983, Paris). Trans. by Mark A. Wauck. San Francisco: Ignatius Press, 1986.
18. Samuel Enoch Stumpf. *Socrates to Sartre: A History of Philosophy.* 5th ed. New York: McGraw-Hill, 1993.

19. Alan W. Watts. *Myth and Ritual in Christianity*. Boston: Beacon Press, 1968.
20. Colin McGinn. "Soul on Fire." *The New Republic* 20 June 1994: 34-39.
21. Richard Weaver. *Ideas Have Consequences*. Chicago: The Univ. of Chicago Press, 1984.

Index

Stevens, Wallace: and the Catholic
  Church, 33; "The Connoisseur of
  Chaos," 33; "The Idea of Order at
  Key West," 3-4; "The Snow Man,"
  1-2
Thomas Aquinas, Thomism, Thomist:
  See Aquinas, Thomas.
Tillich, Paul, 25
Tolkien, J.R.R., 29

Vendler, Helen, 3-4
Vincent, Marvin, 20
Voegelin, Eric, 8
Voices and Visions, 3
Weaver, Richard, 47
Wittgenstein, Ludwig, 47; *Tractatus
  Logico-Philosophicus*, 47
Zeno, 35
zodiac, the, 4